SPAIN

Sarah Tieck

Big Buddy BOOKS
Explore the Countries

VISIT US AT
www.abdopublishing.com

Published by ABDO Publishing Company, PO Box 398166, Minneapolis, MN 55439.

Printed in the United States of America, North Mankato, Minnesota.
052013
092013

♻ PRINTED ON RECYCLED PAPER

Coordinating Series Editor: Rochelle Baltzer
Contributing Editors: Megan M. Gunderson, Marcia Zappa
Graphic Design: Adam Craven
Cover Photograph: *iStockphoto*: ©iStockphoto.com/SOMATUSCANI.
Interior Photographs/Illustrations: *Alamy*: © M.Flynn (p. 17); *AP Photo*: AP Photo (pp. 15, 33), RIA Novosti Kremlin, Mikhail Klimentyev, Presidential Press Service (p. 19), North Wind Picture Archives via AP Images (p. 16), Fabian Stratenschulte/picture-alliance/dpa (p. 35); *Getty Images*: Pablo Blazquez Dominguez (p. 29), Xurxo Lobato (p. 25), Lonely Planet (p. 34); *Glow Images*: © Ullstein Bild (p. 15), imagebroker/Helmut Corneli (p. 23), Ingolf Pompe/LOOK-foto (p. 33); *Shutterstock*: asife (p. 27), S. Borisov (p. 13), Darios (p. 31), FCG (p. 11), Foodpictures (p. 35), Globe Turner (pp. 19, 38), Jack.Q (p. 27), Veniamin Kraskov (p. 35), Maridav (p. 9), Jose Luis Mesa (p. 37), Mikhail Nekrasov (p. 21), Pat_Hastings (p. 34), Maryna Pleshkun (p. 38), Dmitry Sokolov (p. 11), VICTOR TORRES (p. 9), Tupungato (p. 5), Czesznak Zsolt (p. 23).

Country population and area figures taken from the CIA World Factbook.

Library of Congress Control Number: 2013932148

Cataloging-in-Publication Data

Tieck, Sarah.
 Spain / Sarah Tieck.
  p. cm. -- (Explore the countries)
ISBN 978-1-61783-818-7 (lib. bdg.)
1. Spain--Juvenile literature. I. Title.
946--dc23

2013932148

SPAIN

Contents

AROUND THE WORLD

Our world has many countries. Each country has beautiful land. It has its own rich history. And, the people have their own languages and ways of life.

Spain is a country in Europe. What do you know about Spain? Let's learn more about this place and its story!

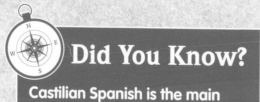

Did You Know?

Castilian Spanish is the main official language in Spain.

Visitors travel to Spain to spend time on its beaches.

PASSPORT TO SPAIN

Spain is a country in southwestern Europe. Three countries border it. It is also bordered by the Atlantic Ocean and the Mediterranean Sea.

Spain's total area is 195,124 square miles (505,370 sq km). More than 47 million people live there.

WHERE IN THE WORLD?

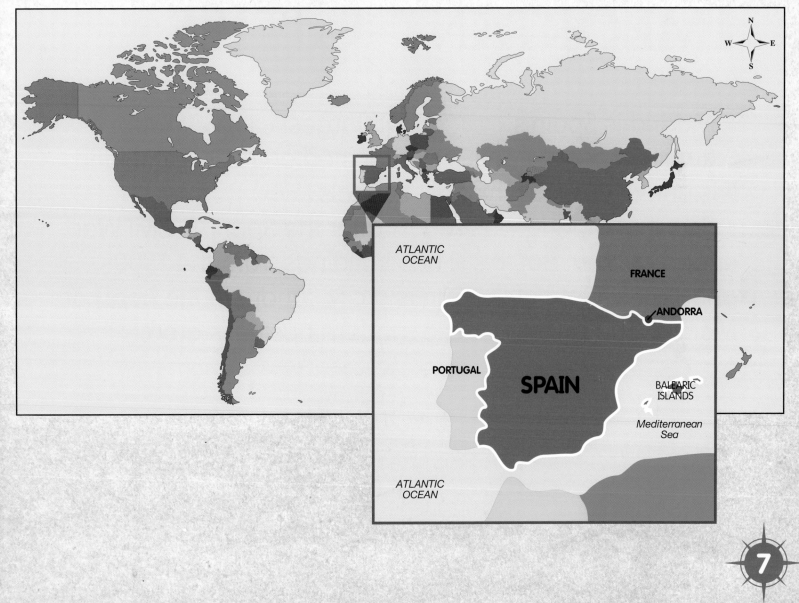

IMPORTANT CITIES

Madrid is Spain's **capital** and largest city, with about 3.2 million people. This city is located on raised, flat land. It is one of Europe's highest capitals.

Some of Madrid was rebuilt after the Spanish Civil War ended in 1939. But, it still has buildings from the 1500s and 1600s. Gate of the Sun is a city square in the heart of Madrid. The city also has a modern business area.

SPAIN

Barcelona

★ Madrid

Valencia

Most people in Madrid live in apartments. There are few houses.

People attend bullfights at Plaza de Toros de Las Ventas in Madrid.

Barcelona is Spain's second-largest city. It has about 1.6 million people. The city is an important manufacturing center and port. Cars, electronics, and cloth are made there.

Valencia is Spain's third-largest city, with nearly 800,000 people. It is known for its history. The Romans built a settlement there around 100 BC. The Moors ruled there from about the AD 700s to the 1200s. They were **Muslims** from northern Africa.

SAY IT

Barcelona
bahr-suh-LOH-nuh

Valencia
vuh-LEHNT-shee-uh

One popular area of Barcelona is Port Vell. People go there to see its aquarium.

The City of Arts and Sciences in Valencia is popular with visitors. There is art, an aquarium, and other exhibits.

Spain in History

People have lived in Spain for thousands of years. Beginning around 200 BC, the Romans ruled Spain for about 600 years. Language, buildings, and roads advanced during this time.

Over the years, many different groups ruled Spain. In the AD 700s, the Moors took over the country.

In the late 1400s, Spain became known for exploration. Its rulers sent explorers to faraway lands. Spain built an **empire** in South America. It also claimed land in Africa, Asia, and Europe. The country grew very wealthy.

The Alhambra was built in Granada by the Moors. This palace is still popular with visitors.

In the 1500s, Spain built a strong **empire**. It was home to many great artists and singers. Beginning in the 1600s, the country began to struggle. And, it was weakened by several wars.

The Spanish Civil War took place from 1936 to 1939. When it ended, Francisco Franco became the country's **dictator**. Spain's businesses grew during this time. In 1978, Spain became a **constitutional monarchy**.

Franco ruled Spain until 1973. He remained the head of state until his death in 1975.

The Spanish Civil War killed many people. And, it changed the government of Spain.

Timeline

1492

Queen Isabella I and King Ferdinand II sent Christopher Columbus on a voyage. He sailed to an island in the Caribbean Sea. He claimed land for Spain.

Around 1043

"El Cid" was born in Vivar. His real name was Rodrigo Diaz de Vivar. He became a famous war hero in Spain.

1519

Hernán Cortés began taking over Mexico for Spain. Spanish rule lasted 300 years in Mexico.

1990

Spanish opera singers José Carreras and Plácido Domingo sang with Italian Luciano Pavarotti in Rome. They formed a group called the Three Tenors.

2010

Sagrada Família opened in Barcelona. Antoni Gaudí worked on the design until his death in 1926. Building on this church began around 1883. It continues today.

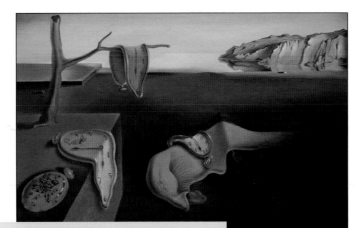

1931

Salvador Dalí painted *The Persistence of Memory*. This famous painting is in a style called **surrealism**. The rocks were inspired by Catalonia, his homeland.

An Important Symbol

The design for Spain's flag was first introduced in 1785. The current version was adopted in 1981. It has two red stripes and one yellow stripe. The state flag includes a coat of arms. The people's flag just has the three stripes.

Spain's government is a **constitutional monarchy**. The parliament makes laws. The king or queen is the head of state. The prime minister is the head of government.

The coat of arms has a shield with symbols. They stand for Spain's historic kingdoms.

Juan Carlos I became the king of Spain in 1975.

ACROSS THE LAND

Spain has mountains, coasts, forests, plains, and islands. Much of the country is high, dry plains. Mountain systems include the Pyrenees and the Cantabrian.

Spain is known for its sunny beaches. The Balearic Islands and Canary Islands are part of Spain.

Major rivers in Spain include the Tagus and Ebro. The **Strait** of Gibraltar separates Spain from Africa.

Did You Know?

In January, the average temperature in central Spain is below 30°F (-1°C). In July, it is above 80°F (27°C).

One of Spain's longest rivers is the Tagus. It flows 626 miles (1,007 km) to the Atlantic Ocean.

Many types of animals make their homes in Spain. These include wolves, lynx, hares, wild boars, and brown bears. Squid, swordfish, mussels, eels, and sardines live in the coastal waters.

Spain's land is home to many different plants. Evergreen oak, beech, pine, and poplar trees grow there.

Some people hunt wild boars in Spain.

Mediterranean morays are a type of eel. They are found off the coast of Spain.

Earning a Living

Spain makes important products. These include cars, wine, and food. Many people work in the country's factories. Others have service jobs, such as helping visitors to Spain.

Spain has valuable natural **resources**. Iron ore is mined there. Farmers produce sugar beets, oranges, olives, and tomatoes. They raise cattle, pigs, poultry, and sheep. Some pigs are raised to make Spain's famous serrano ham.

LIFE IN SPAIN

Spain is famous for its sunny land. People in Spain spend much of their time outdoors. They gather with friends and enjoy long meals. Spain is also known for its artists, musicians, and filmmakers.

Traditional Spanish foods include paella, churros, and gazpacho. People drink strong coffee, hot chocolate, wine, and sangria.

Did You Know?

In Spain, children must attend school from ages 6 to 16.

Flamenco music and dance is popular in Spain.

Paella includes seafood, meats, vegetables, and rice. It is prepared and served in a special pan.

The Spanish enjoy football, or soccer. They watch matches in large stadiums. People also watch bullfights. Other favorite activities are spending time at the beach and in sidewalk cafés.

Most Spanish people belong to the Roman Catholic Church. Many holidays are connected to religion. Before Easter, some cities and villages honor **Holy** Week with parades.

A famous event called the running of the bulls happens every July in Pamplona. People try to dodge bulls as they run down the streets!

29

FAMOUS FACES

Many talented people are from Spain. Miguel de Cervantes was a writer. He was born around September 29, 1547, in Alcalá de Henares. He died in 1616.

Cervantes wrote poems, plays, and novels. His most famous work is a novel called *Don Quixote*. It was printed in two parts in 1605 and 1615. It is about an ordinary man who believes that he is a knight.

SAY IT

Miguel de Cervantes
mih-GEHL day suhr-VAN-tees

A monument in Madrid honors Cervantes. The statues show Cervantes and characters from *Don Quixote*.

Did You Know?

In 1575, Cervantes was captured by pirates and made a slave. He was captive for five years. His experience gave him ideas for *Don Quixote*.

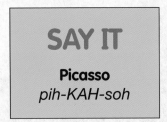
Spain is known for its artists, including Pablo Picasso. He was born in Málaga on October 25, 1881. His work greatly **influenced** modern art.

Picasso is known for a painting style called cubism. In 1937, he painted *Guernica*. This painting is 25.5 feet (7.8 m) long! It is about war and suffering. Picasso created many more pieces of art before his death in 1973.

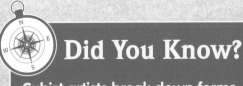

Did You Know?

Cubist artists break down forms into basic shapes and signs. Then, they combine them in new ways.

Guernica is in the Queen Sofía Museum in Madrid. It helps people around the world learn about the Spanish Civil War.

Picasso painted, sculpted, and made ceramics. He even designed theater stages.

Tour Book

Have you ever been to Spain? If you visit the country, here are some places to go and things to do!

Hear

Experience musical plays. Zarzuela is a type of light, funny opera that started in Spain in the 1600s.

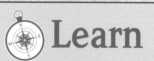
Learn

Visit the Museo del Prado in Madrid. Many famous works of art are displayed there.

 ## Cheer

Take in a soccer game. Real Madrid is a favorite team based in Madrid.

Eat

Share some snacks, or tapas. These include cold and hot foods. Common tapas are Spanish omelets, fried squid, and olives.

 ## Explore

Visit Sagrada Família. Construction is ongoing. But, visitors can still see many parts of this large church and attend its services. Some say it is one of Spain's greatest buildings.

A GREAT COUNTRY

The story of Spain is important to our world. The people and places that make up this country offer something special. They help make the world a more beautiful, interesting place.

Sevilla's cathedral is one of the largest churches in Europe. It has a tower that is more than 300 feet (90 m) high.

Spain Up Close

Official Name: Reino de España (Kingdom of Spain)

Flag:

Population (rank): 47,042,984 (July 2012 est.) (27th most-populated country)

Total Area (rank): 195,124 square miles (52nd largest country)

Capital: Madrid

Official Language: Castilian Spanish

Currency: Euro

Form of Government: Constitutional monarchy

National Anthem: "Marcha Real" (The Royal March)

Important Words

capital a city where government leaders meet.
constitutional monarchy a form of government in which a king or queen has only those powers given by a country's laws and constitution.
dictator a ruler with complete control.
empire a large group of states or countries under one ruler called an emperor or empress.
holy important to a religion.
influence to have an effect on something without the direct use of force.
Muslim a person who practices Islam, which is a religion based on a belief in Allah as God and Muhammad as his prophet.
resource a supply of something useful or valued.
strait a narrow waterway connecting two larger bodies of water.
surrealism a style of art that combines images in a dreamlike or strange way.

Web Sites

To learn more about Spain, visit ABDO Publishing Company online. Web sites about Spain are featured on our Book Links page. These links are routinely monitored and updated to provide the most current information available.

www.abdopublishing.com

Index